W9-AFI-556

WHAT WOULD YOU CHOOSE?

RUN AS FAST AS USAIN BOLT OR...

...SMASH AS HARD AS SERENA WILLIAMS ?

SUPERSPORTS

HELEN GREATHEAD

 Gareth Stevens
PUBLISHING

Please visit our website, www.garethstevens.com.
For a free color catalog of all our high-quality books,
call toll free 1-800-542-2595 or fax 1-877-542-2596.

Cataloging-in-Publication Data

Names: Greathead, Helen.
Title: Supersports / Helen Greathead.
Description: New York : Gareth Stevens Publishing, 2017. | Series: What would you choose?| Includes index.
Identifiers: ISBN 9781482461183 (pbk.) | ISBN 9781482461787 (library bound) | ISBN 9781482461190 (6 pack)
Subjects: LCSH: Sports--Miscellanea--Juvenile literature.
Classification: LCC GV707.G724 2017 | DDC 796--d23

Published in 2017 by Gareth Stevens Publishing
111 East 14th Street, Suite 349
New York, NY 10003

Series editor: Adrian Cole
Art direction: Peter Scoulding
Series designer: D. R. ink
Picture researcher: Diana Morris

Photo credits Accent Alaska/Alamy: 11t. Thomas Barrat/Shutterstock: 25cr. Michal Bednarek/Dreamstime: 22. Lasse Behnke/Dreamstime: 13bl. Lance Bellers/Shutterstock: back cover bl. Adam Blascik/Dreamstime: 5br. Blitzkoenig/ Dreamstime: 20b. S Burel/Dreamstime: 18. Byelikova/Dreamstime: 17b. Rich Carey/Shutterstock: front cover r. Jaromir Chalabala/Dreamstime: 12c. Amos Chapple/Rex Shutterstock: 16b. John Coletti/Getty Images: 10b. Marcin Bartosz Czarnoleski/Dreamstime: 8c. Dole Plantation: 13t.Chad Ehlers/Alamy: 9t. Richard Ellis/Alamy: 15t. Javier Etcheverry/ Alamy: 26b. Steffen Foerster/Shutterstock: 10c. Karen Foley/Dreamstime: 24b. Victor Habbick/Shutterstock 8t. Birgit Reitz-Hofmann/Shutterstock: 30bl. irisphoto1/Shutterstock: 5c. Alan Jeffrey/Dreamstime: 5bl. Kacmerka/Dreamstime: 12tr. Jaroslaw Killian/Dreamstime: 19bl. Yongyut Kimsry/Shutterstock: 23. Jan Kranendonk/Dreamstime: 20tl. Rafal Kubiak/ Shutterstock: 29. Alex Lauer/Dreamstime: 8br. Henrik Lehnerer/NASA/Shutterstock: front cover l. Mmeeds/Dreamstime: 14bl, 14br. Marian Mocanu/Dreamstime: 27c. Alex Mourant/Caters News Agency: 24t. NASA: 7b, 12tl, 27tl, 27tr. Courtesy of NOAA/Institute for Exploration/University of Rhode Island (NOAA/IFE/URI/wikimedia commons: 19b. Nico Nomad/ Shutterstock: front cover c. Ruth Eastham & Max Paoli/Getty Images: 13cl. Paul Parker/SPL: 30cl. William Perugini/ Shutterstock: 20tr. Philcold/Dreamstime: 13br. Patrick Poendl/Dreamstime: 8bl. Povarov/Dreamstime: 27b. Quirky China News/Rex Shutterstock: 16cb. Radekdrewek/Dreamstime: 16t. Rsazonov/Dreamstime: 21bl. Hugo Rosseels/Dreamstime: 30tr. Scaliger/Dreamstime: 30cr. Sergeyussr/Dreamstime: 26t. Sipa Press/Rex Shutterstock: 17t. Harald Slauschek/Getty Images: 6b. Smandy/Dreamstime: 21br. Alex Streinu/Dreamstime: 25b. Nimon Thong-uthai/Dreamstime: 12bl. 3D sculptor/ Shutterstock: back cover t. Waitomo Glowworm Caves: 20cr. Patrick Ward/Alamy: 9c. Wead/Shutterstock: back cover br. Isabella Wertschnig/Shutterstock: 16c. Wisconsin Art/Dreamstime: 28. Paul Ziklia/Dreamstime: 5t.

Printed in the United States of America

CPSIA compliance information: Batch CW17GS: For further information contact Gareth Stevens, New York, New York at 1-800-542-2595.

CONTENTS

WOULD YOU CHOOSE

TO SHOOT AT GOAL LIKE PELÉ, RACE IN A HOLLOWED-OUT PUMPKIN OR GO SNORKELING … IN A BOG?

Supersports invites you to find out about some sports you'd most like to run, hop, skip, swim or jump your way into and make some tricky decisions.

Read each question,

CONSIDER YOUR OPTIONS,

check out the facts,

see what your friends think (and what we chose) and then make YOUR choice.

WHAT WOULD YOU CHOOSE?

HIT A RUBBER BALL FAST IN SQUASH ... OR A SHUTTLECOCK FAST IN BADMINTON?

WE CHOSE

Badminton. Both games are speedy. You can burn 1,000 calories in one hour of squash, and run 4 miles (6.4 km) during a game of badminton. A squash ball can travel at up to 170 miles per hour (274 km/h), but 2013 saw a new Guinness World Record for a badminton smash — 306 miles per hour (492 km/h)! Badminton is the fastest racket sport in the world.

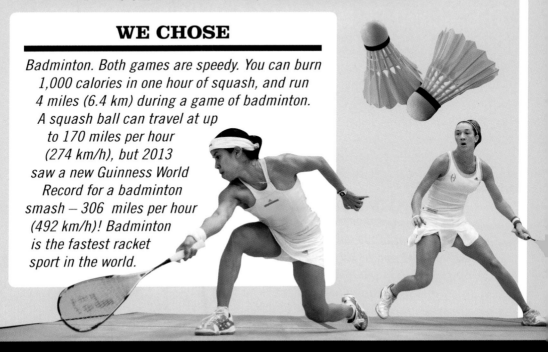

HAVE AN "ENDO" IN A CYCLE RACE... OR "CHIN" IN A BOXING MATCH?

WE CHOSE

Have chin. If someone says you've got "chin" in boxing, they're paying you a compliment. It means you can stay standing even after a potential knockout blow. In cycling, if you've had an "endo" you've tipped over the handlebars!

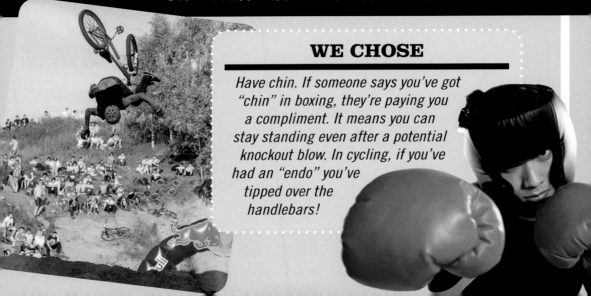

RUN ALONG THE GREAT WALL OF CHINA ... OR TO THE ISLAND OF MONT SAINT MICHEL IN FRANCE?

The Great Wall Marathon accepts 2,500 runners from 60 different countries. As well as running along China's most famous landmark, you'll pass through villages, fields and farmland, with encouragement and refreshments provided by local people.

The Mont Saint Michel Marathon in France crosses from Brittany into Normandy. Up to 5,000 runners from over 30 countries take part. You'll run along the coast, through villages and beautiful countryside.

AND FINALLY ...

The Great Wall Marathon is one of the hardest in the world, with steep climbs and descents that include over 5,000 steps! Plus, if you fail to return to the Great Wall within six hours, you'll be disqualified. In the Mont Saint Michel Marathon you'll race against time to cross the beach and reach the island before the tide comes in!

WE CHOSE

France. You'll see the island finish point when you start, which means that this course is mostly flat — phew!

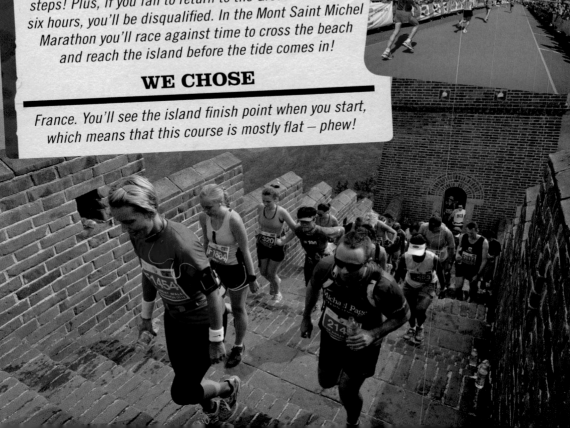

WHAT WOULD YOU CHOOSE?

SLIDE DOWN AN ICY TRACK IN THE LUGE ... OR THE SKELETON AT THE WINTER OLYMPICS?

WE CHOSE

The luge. In both sports the sled has no brakes, and you'll career down the steep, curved track at around 87 miles per hour (140 km/h). In the luge (left), you'll travel feet first, pushing off from your sled, but in the skeleton (top) you run along the ice, jump onto the sled and then travel headfirst, facedown, hoping to avoid a collision!

SCORE "LOVE" IN TENNIS ... OR A "CONDOR" IN GOLF?

WE CHOSE

The condor. "Love" in tennis means a big fat zero, but in golf a "condor" is the rarest result you can get. It happens if you hit the ball into the hole in one shot, when the course says a good golfer would do it in five. Hardly anyone has ever scored a condor!

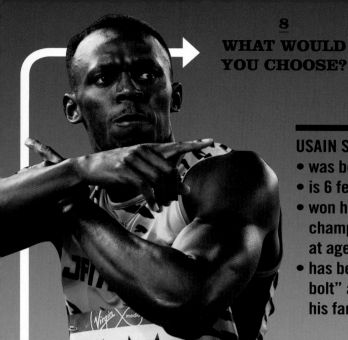

THE FACTS

USAIN ST. LEO BOLT:
- was born in Jamaica in 1986
- is 6 feet 5 inches (1.96 m) tall
- won his first world championship, running 200 m, at age just 15
- has been nicknamed "lightning bolt" and celebrates a win with his famous lightning bolt pose

RUN AS FAST AS USAIN BOLT …
OR SMASH AS HARD AS SERENA WILLIAMS?

SO USAIN'S BEEN RUNNING SINCE HE WAS A KID?

Usain won his first track and field medals at age 14, for the hurdles and the high jump. He moved onto running the 200 m and 400 m, and he didn't compete in the 100 m until 2007.

WHAT ELSE HAS USAIN WON?

At the 2008 Beijing Olympics he won gold medals in the 100 m, 200 m and 4×100 m relay, setting new world records in each event. At the 2012 London Olympics and the 2016 Rio Olympics, he won gold in the same three events!

Didn't you know?
Usain Bolt can run at a top speed of 27.7 miles per hour (44.7 km/h)!

THE FACTS

SERENA JAMEKA WILLIAMS:
- was born in Michigan, USA, in 1981
- is 5 feet 9 inches (1.75 m) tall
- turned professional at the age of 14
- is the youngest of five sisters

Didn't you know?
You get a Grand Slam title for winning any of these top tennis competitions: the Australian Open, Roland Garros (French Open), Wimbledon and US Open.

SO SERENA HAS BEEN PLAYING TENNIS SINCE SHE WAS A KID?

Serena was just three years old when she had her first tennis lesson with her dad. She practiced for two hours a day against her older sister, Venus. The family moved to Florida to find better coaching for the girls, who turned professional in 1995.

SO WHAT ELSE HAS SHE WON?

At age 17, Serena won the US Open women's singles title, and by 2015 she had 21 Grand Slam titles under her belt for singles alone. In 2012, she won four Olympic gold medals in women's doubles and singles. Of course, she's helped by her powerful serve, which travels up to 129 miles per hour (207 km/h)!

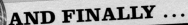

AND FINALLY ...

Fans say Serena has brought athleticism and power to women's tennis, and that she's the best women's tennis player ever. She's been a champion for 20 years and her serve is starting to slow in favor of accurate positioning. Fans of Usain say his technique can still improve and he could run 100 m in 9.4 seconds!

WE CHOSE

Usain — who wouldn't want to be the fastest person in the world?

WRESTLE IN WWE ...
OR THE ANCIENT
MARTIAL ART
OF PANKRATION?

WE CHOSE

WWE (World Wrestling Entertainment). It's just for show, with both wrestlers following rehearsed moves. Most injuries in WWE are actually fake. Pankration, however, was a mixture of boxing and wrestling, and it was very real! There were only two rules: no gouging (of eyes, nose or mouth) and no biting. You'd fight naked, and you might only win if your opponent died!

TAKE UP CHEERLEADING ...
OR SYNCHRONIZED SWIMMING?

WE CHOSE

Synchronized swimming. "Synchro" isn't just swimming, it also involves acrobatics and dance. You can't touch the bottom of the pool, and have to do some moves underwater while holding your breath for up to three minutes! Cheerleading demands strength, poise, flexibility and the ability to do stunts — your teammates might throw you 20 feet (6 m) into the air! In the US, 70 percent of all serious injuries among female student athletes are due to cheerleading.

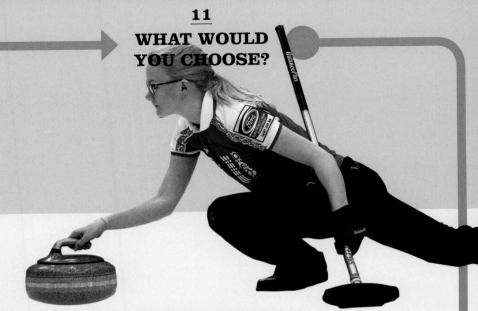

TRY YOUR HAND AT IRISH HURLING ... OR SCOTTISH CURLING?

Hurling is an Irish field sport that's been played for over 800 years. You'll carry a paddle-like stick (hurley) and chase a small leather ball (sliotar). You can kick the ball, hit it with your hand or stick, and even carry it on the stick. Score one point for getting the ball over the H-shaped post, and three for getting it into the net.

Curling has been popular since the 16th century. You'll play on ice, sliding a 40-pound (18 kg) stone with a handle on the top towards the center of a marked circle (house). The team with their stones closest to the house wins. Players "sweep" the ice to smooth it, helping the stones travel further.

AND FINALLY ...

Hurling is a men-only sport (women play the sport of camogie). Youth players have a helmet to protect their head but nothing to shield them from a whack on the shins! Curling rules are easy to learn, you don't need to skate and anyone can play.

WE CHOSE

Curling. The only thing to get whacked are the stones!

WHAT WOULD YOU CHOOSE?

TEST YOURSELF TO THE MAX IN THE VENDÉE GLOBE YACHT RACE ... OR THE TOUR DE FRANCE CYCLE RACE?

THE FACTS

THE VENDÉE GLOBE YACHT RACE:

- first took place in 1989 to commemorate Joshua Slocum's single-handed circumnavigation of the globe in 1895
- happens every four years; it'll take up to three months to travel over 27,000 miles (44,000 km), depending on how well you sail
- fastest finish was in 2013, when François Gabart completed it in 78 days, 2 hours and 16 minutes

SO WHAT DO I DO IN THE VENDÉE?

You'll be competing against up to 24 others, and sailing solo from the French coast, down the Atlantic, across the Antarctic and Pacific Oceans, then back up the Atlantic. First to the finish, without stopping or asking for help, is the winner.

WHAT SORT OF BOAT WILL I NEED?

A modern racing yacht that's lightweight, but also strong, watertight and unsinkable — plus a sponsor to pay for it. The boat will be around 62 feet (19 m) long, with a 92-foot (28 m) mast — and if there's a problem, whatever the weather, it'll be you who climbs up to repair it!

Didn't you know?
Thirteen skippers entered the first ever race in 1989. Only seven finished: four boats were damaged, one retired after requiring help, and one sailor was forced to quit because of a toothache!

Didn't you know? It's essential to keep eating on the Tour, as you'll burn up to 8,000 calories a day!

WHAT ABOUT THE TOUR DE FRANCE?

You'll be part of a team of nine cyclists that will cover up to 140 miles (225 km) per day, in 21 stages. Each stage winner wears the yellow jersey. The overall winner is the cyclist with the fastest time.

WHAT SORT OF BIKE DO I NEED?

A specially made road bike that's aerodynamic and strong, but lightweight. Rules restrict the weight to at least 15 pounds (6.8 kg), and the type of handlebar, pedal and seat post you can use. You'll need the right helmet too, and even your socks must be the right length!

THE FACTS

THE TOUR DE FRANCE:
- first took place in 1903 to promote a French sports newspaper; it's happened every year since, except during the two World Wars
- is around 2,175 miles (3,500 km) long and takes three weeks to complete
- has flat, mountain and speed stages; winners in the different categories get to wear special jerseys

AND FINALLY ...

In the Tour, you'll cycle up to 5.5 hours a day with the support of your team, your leader and over 12 million spectators along the route. In the Vendée you'll be completely alone, with no days off, no one to crew or cook for you and just 5 hours of sleep a night.

WE CHOSE

The Tour de France. There's a much greater chance you'll actually finish!

CHEER ON PLAYERS IN A FICTION-INSPIRED GAME OF CHESSBOXING ... OR QUIDDITCH?

Chessboxing starts with a timed round of chess on a table in a boxing ring. When the bell sounds, the table is cleared away and the boxing begins. There are 11 rounds in total, but the game can finish sooner if a player gives up, gets checkmate or knocks out their opponent.

Quidditch is a cross between rugby and handball — but with a broom between your legs! Each team has seven players: three can score goals; two try to take out opposing players; the keeper guards their goal hoop, and the seeker chases the human snitch!

AND FINALLY ...

... Chessboxing first appeared in a graphic novel. Combining the two ancient sports is an all-out physical and mental test. The quidditch match isn't quite like the one played by Harry Potter. Real-life games are only open to muggles so, sadly, there's no flying involved.

WE CHOSE

Chessboxing. Fans say it could be an Olympic sport by 2024!

TAKE UP SEPAK TAKRAW FROM MALAYSIA ... OR BOSSABALL FROM SPAIN?

Sepak Takraw (top right) is a cross between soccer and volleyball. Two teams of three players hit the ball up to three times to get it over a high net, without using their hands. The first team to reach an agreed score, of 15 or 21, wins the set.

Bossaball is like volleyball too, but you can use any part of your body and up to five hits to get the ball over the net. You'll play on a huge inflatable pitch, with trampolines on either side of the net! Teams of 4 or 5 players need to score 25 points, with a two-point lead, to win.

AND FINALLY ...

Bossaball is great fun, but requires inflatable equipment. Sepak Takraw is the fastest-growing sport in Asia, but it's already over 500 years old.

WE CHOSE

Sepak Takraw. It's great for stretching your legs!

BE A SHORT BASKETBALL PLAYER ...
OR A TALL JOCKEY?

THE FACTS

BASKETBALL:

- was invented in 1891 by a Canadian PE instructor working at a YMCA training school
- goals were originally peach boxes (with no hole in the bottom until 1903!); they still stand 10 feet (3 m) off the ground
- became an Olympic sport in 1936

DO BASKETBALL PLAYERS HAVE TO BE TALL?

Being tall is definitely desirable. The average height of a basketball player in the National Basketball Association (NBA) increased from 6 feet 2 inches (1.88 m) in 1947 to 6 feet 7 inches (2 m) in 2016. In 2014, English team Cheshire Phoenix signed the tallest player in the world, Paul Sturgess (left), who is 7 feet 7 inches (2.32 m)!

HOW DO TALL PLAYERS FIT INTO A TEAM?

The tallest players are usually centers, who stay close to the basket. Forwards come next. Guards are usually the shortest players. They need to be able to dribble fast and pass the ball, setting up the play for a shot on goal.

THE FACTS

HORSE RACING:
- can include steeplechases, point-to-point, hurdle races and flat races (without jumps)
- is one of the world's oldest sports and has hardly changed for centuries
- can involve different distances and numbers of horses, but each race is won by the first horse and rider across the finishing line

DO JOCKEYS HAVE TO BE SHORT?

It's not so much the height of the rider that matters, as the weight. Before each race, jockeys have to be weighed to make sure each horse is carrying an appropriate load for its age. There have been weight guidelines for jockeys since the 1850s.

WHAT'S THE IDEAL HEIGHT?

The ideal height is 5 feet 5 inches to 5 feet 9 inches (1.65–1.76 m), though there aren't any height restrictions. The US's shortest jockey was Julie Krone, at 4 feet 10½ inches (1.49 m), while British jockey George Baker is 5 feet 11½ inches (1.82 m) tall, and Danish jockey Louise Moeller is 6 feet 1 inch (1.85 m)!

AND FINALLY ...

Muggsy Bogues had a successful career in US basketball even though he was only 5 feet 3 inches (1.6 m) tall. Jockeys of all sizes have to keep their weight down — Louise Moeller rides at just 110 pounds (50 kg) — but this can result in health-threatening diets.

WE CHOSE

Basketball. Who wants to have to skip meals?

SNORKEL THROUGH A BOG ...
OR RACE AGAINST A HORSE?

Bog snorkelers wear goggles and fins as well as a snorkel, and are timed as they navigate 436 feet (133 m) of freezing, filthy water in trenches that are cut into the bog. The fastest time wins, but there's a catch: you can't use conventional swimming strokes.

In 2014, over 600 runners raced against 50 horses and riders in the Man vs. Horse race. People get a 15-minute head start on the grueling 23.6-mile (38 km) run that's dotted with hills, crags, bogs — and fast-moving horses. It's easiest to run as part of a three-person relay team.

AND FINALLY ...

In 35 years, only two people have ever run faster than a horse. Though it's tough, the snorkeling doesn't last long. The 2014 record was 1 minute 22 seconds. Racing against a horse, on the other hand, takes the average single runner over 4 hours to complete.

WE CHOSE

Snorkeling. You have more chance of winning!

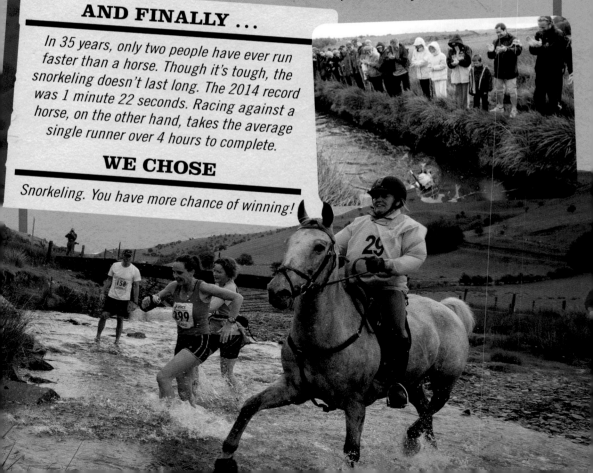

TAKE PART IN AN 1830s GAME OF SOCCER ...
OR CRICKET?

WE CHOSE

Cricket. The rules for cricket were written down in 1744: bowlers weren't allowed to raise their arm above their shoulder, so the ball didn't travel as fast as it does today. Before 1863, however, there were no rules or referees in soccer; it was a very dangerous game!

DO A FOSBURY FLOP
IN THE HIGH JUMP ...
OR HAVE A FALSE START
IN AN OLYMPIC SPRINT?

WE CHOSE

The Fosbury Flop. Dick Fosbury's technique of going backwards over the high-jump bar shocked officials during the 1968 Olympics, but he wasn't disqualified — he cleared 7 feet 4¼ inches (2.24 m) and won himself a gold medal. Most great high jumpers still use his technique today. One false start will disqualify you from an Olympic race.

PUNCH LIKE ALI ... OR SHOOT LIKE PELÉ?

THE FACTS

MUHAMMAD ALI:
- was born Cassius Marcellus Clay Junior in Louisville, Kentucky, in 1942
- took up boxing at age 12 after his bicycle was stolen (so he could beat up the person who took it)
- changed his name to Muhammad Ali in 1964, after converting to Islam

SO HOW DID ALI FIGHT?

Ali kept his hands low, his feet moving and his anger under control. He was good at taking or dodging punches, and delivering them! He often let his opponents throw punches at him, so they exhausted themselves, before he'd hit back.

HOW GOOD WAS HE?

Ali won 56 bouts and lost 5. He won light heavyweight gold at the 1960 Olympics, and was World Heavyweight Boxing Champion three times (no one else had achieved this).

Didn't you know?

Ali famously won the "Rumble in the Jungle" boxing match against George Foreman, in Zaire (now the DRC) in 1974. At that time he was said to be the most recognizable person in the world!

SO HOW DID PELÉ PLAY?

Pelé was a great athlete who could do everything. He used tricks he'd learned on the streets to dribble and swerve around his opponents.

HE MUST HAVE SCORED SOME GREAT GOALS

His first professional goal was for Santos, at 16. At age 17 he became the youngest player ever to score in a World Cup, and at age 30 he scored Brazil's 100th World Cup goal. He was hailed as the best player in the world at just 21, and in over 1,366 career matches, he scored 1,282 goals.

THE FACTS

PELÉ:
- **was born in 1940 in Brazil; his real name is Edson Arantes do Nascimento**
- **started out kicking a sock stuffed with rags around the local streets and at age nine, he promised his dad he would win the World Cup**
- **was expelled from school for kicking a ball during schooltime**

AND FINALLY ...

Because of Ali's impact on the sport, and because he beat so many great boxers, he is considered the greatest heavyweight boxer of all time. Some say other footballers who played for Brazil were just as good as Pelé.

WE CHOSE

Punch like Ali – he was voted BBC Sports Personality of the Century in 1999, winning as many votes as the other four contenders (including Pelé) put together.

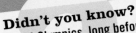

Didn't you know?
At the 1904 Olympics, long before the Paralympics began, German-born George Eyser won the gold for rope climbing, despite having a wooden leg. He won five other medals, too.

CLIMB A ROPE ... OR SKIP WITH IT?

WE CHOSE

Skipping. It is quick and easy to master — boxers do it to build up their stamina. It's said that ten minutes of skipping can be as effective as a 30-minute run!

CHALLENGE CRISTIANO RONALDO ... OR MILENE DOMINGUES TO A KEEPY UPPY CONTEST?

WE CHOSE

Cristiano Ronaldo. You're more likely to beat the soccer legend. Milene Domingues broke the keepy uppy World Record in 1997. She kicked a ball 55,187 times without letting it touch the floor (balancing it on the back of her neck for bathroom breaks!).

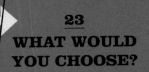

TOSS A HAMMER ... OR A TUNA FISH?

The hammer you'll throw is actually a solid ball of metal with a wire handle and weighs up to 15.9 pounds (7.2 kg). You'll swing it around your head several times before spinning your body around three or four times, and letting the hammer fly. It must land in the right part of the field. The furthest throw wins.

The tuna toss takes place each January at the Tunarama Festival in Port Lincoln, Australia. Mostly you'll toss a rubber fish, in much the same way as you'd throw the hammer. But in the finals you'll toss a real frozen 17.6-pound (8 kg) tuna fish, with a rope handle.

Didn't you know?
If tuna tossing isn't to your taste, other Tunarama events include prawn peeling and a watermelon-eating contest.

AND FINALLY ...

Hammer throwing is a 3,000-year-old sport that probably started using chariot wheels. Tunarama started in 1979, as a way to highlight the local fishing industry. You're more likely to win the tuna toss, where the record is 122.1 feet (37.23 m). The current men's world hammer-throwing record is 284.6 feet (86.74 m) and the women's is 266 feet (81.08 m).

WE CHOSE

The tuna. Even if you don't win the tuna toss, you'll still get lunch.

ENTER THE TOUGH MUDDER CHALLENGE ... OR THE ZOMBIE EVACUATION RACE?

"Tough Mudder" obstacle courses (bottom) are designed to test your mental and physical strength. The courses change every year, but you might find yourself wading waist-deep in mud or scaling a 10-foot (3 m) wall.

In the "Zombie Evacuation Race" you really will be escaping from zombies, with all kinds of objects you'll have to run, climb, jump over — or even throw. You'll be given a belt with three "lives" attached. If the zombies get all of them, you'll be classified as "infected."

AND FINALLY ...

The Tough Mudder is a grueling 10–12.5 miles (16–20 km) long, with obstacles all the way. You aim to finish rather than win, and you sign a death waiver before you start! The Zombie Evacuation is only 3.1 miles (5 km) long.

WE CHOSE

Zombie Evacuation. If you lose all of your lives you'll be invited back next year as a zombie!

RACE AFTER A WHEEL OF CHEESE ...
OR IN A GIANT PUMPKIN?

People have been chasing cheeses down Cooper's Hill in Gloucester, UK, for well over 200 years. The wheel of cheese weighs around 6.6 pounds (3 kg). Runners race after the cheese and whoever gets to the bottom of the very steep hill first (or catches the cheese) wins the race (and the cheese).

Giant Pumpkin kayaking has been happening in Nova Scotia, Canada, for over 15 years. Some of the world's largest pumpkins have been grown there. Contestants weigh their pumpkin and hollow it out on the spot, before paddling it across the lake.

AND FINALLY ...

The local council warns people to stay away from the cheese-rolling contest because of safety issues. The hill is very steep and bones are often broken and muscles sprained. One wrong move carving your pumpkin and you could be bailing out water.

WE CHOSE

Pumpkin paddling. Watch as others chase the cheese (or you could take part in the under-14s uphill race.)

SNOWBOARD LIKE SHAUN WHITE ...
OR SKATEBOARD LIKE TONY HAWK?

THE FACTS

SHAUN ROGER WHITE:
- was born in San Diego, in 1986
- was nicknamed "Future Boy," then the "Flying Tomato" (because of his long red hair)
- won his first snowboarding contest at the age of seven and turned professional at 13

SO SHAUN WAS A TALENTED KID?

Yes, even though he'd had to have surgery for a heart problem. Shaun was skiing at just age four, but at six he switched to snowboarding — his mom hoped it would slow him down. However, Shaun was racing and jumping before the end of his first day on the board.

JUST HOW GOOD IS HE?

Shaun started out jumping higher than other snowboarders, and quickly added in twists and turns. At 17 he won the men's slope-style and superpipe competition in his first Winter X Games. He won consecutive gold medals in the half-pipe at the 2006 and 2010 Winter Olympics.

WHAT WOULD YOU CHOOSE?

SO TONY WAS TALENTED?

Yes, Tony did well at school, but didn't really fit in. By the age of 16 he was already the best competitive skater in the world. At 25, he had entered 103 professional contests, won 73 of them and come second in 19.

JUST HOW GOOD IS HE?

Tony was vertical skateboard champion for 12 years in a row. He invented over 80 skateboard tricks and became a legend, after the X Games in 1999, as the first person ever to land a "900" (spinning two and a half times in the air).

THE FACTS

TONY (ANTHONY FRANK) HAWK:
- was born in San Diego, in 1968
- is nicknamed "Birdman" because of his last name
- started winning local contests when he was 12 and turned professional at 14

AND FINALLY ...

Today Tony is one of most recognizable athletes in the US. If skateboarding had been an Olympic sport, he'd certainly have a few medals. Shaun on the other hand doesn't just snowboard, he's great on a skateboard, too. He was the first competitor to enter (and win medals in) both the Winter and Summer X Games.

WE CHOSE

Shaun White — especially if, like Shaun, you get Tony Hawk as your skateboarding mentor!

TRY A GAME OF PÉTANQUE … OR CROQUET?

In pétanque each player needs three boules (balls). Standing in a circle, team one throws the small wooden ball (the "jack"), then players from each team take turns to throw their boules as close to the jack as possible. Points are scored for landing nearest.

To play croquet, players take turns to knock their colored balls through 12 metal hoops, aiming to hit the peg at the end. Points are scored for the number of hoops you pass through and for hitting the peg.

Didn't you know?

Pétanque came from the age-old French game of boules (bowls). In 14th-century France, poor people weren't allowed to play!

AND FINALLY …

Today, 17 million people play pétanque in France, and it's popular in 52 countries around the world. Croquet is mostly played in the UK, US, Australia and New Zealand. You don't have to be posh to play, but you do need a very flat lawn.

WE CHOSE

Pétanque. You can play almost anywhere.

ACE THREE SPORTS IN A TRIATHLON ... OR SEVEN IN THE HEPTATHLON?

In an Olympic triathlon you'll swim 0.9 miles (1.5 km), cycle 25 miles (40 km) and run 6.2 miles (10 km) in one go, but different events involve different distances. The Ironman has a 2.4-mile (3.86 km) swim and 112-mile (180 km) cycle with a marathon, a 26.2-mile (42.2 km) run, to finish! Above all, you'll need to pace yourself.

The Olympic heptathlon is a two-day women's event that includes 100 m hurdles, high jump, shot put, a 200 m run, long jump, javelin and an 800 m run (phew!). The longest event comes last — when you're most exhausted!

AND FINALLY ...

You'll have to train hard for the heptathlon to master all the sporting skills. The triathlon is becoming much more popular, but it's a real test of endurance.

WE CHOSE

Heptathlon — who wants to ride a bike in wet pants?

WHAT WOULD YOU CHOOSE?

ENTER THE SPRINGBOARD CHOP ... OR THE HOT SAW IN THE LUMBERJACK GAMES?

WE CHOSE

The hot saw. In this event you'll saw off three slices of a tree trunk with a chainsaw as quickly as possible (left). In the springboard chop you'll hack a groove into a tree trunk, wedge a plank of wood in the notch, then balance on it as you chop through a wooden block on top of the trunk — yikes!

BREAK AN ANIMAL SPORTS RECORD WITH A SNAIL ... OR A FROG?

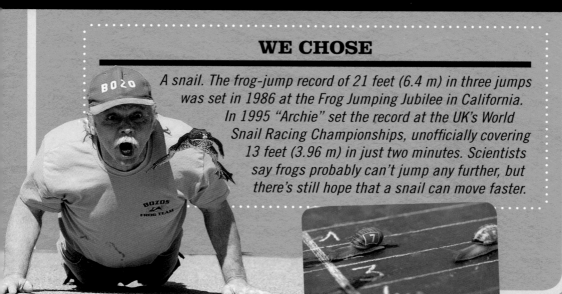

WE CHOSE

A snail. The frog-jump record of 21 feet (6.4 m) in three jumps was set in 1986 at the Frog Jumping Jubilee in California. In 1995 "Archie" set the record at the UK's World Snail Racing Championships, unofficially covering 13 feet (3.96 m) in just two minutes. Scientists say frogs probably can't jump any further, but there's still hope that a snail can move faster.

WHAT WOULD YOU CHOOSE?

GLOSSARY

aerodynamic – Having a shape that reduces the drag from air moving past.

athletics – Sports which take place on a track or field, such as running races, jumping or throwing.

bog – An area of wet, muddy ground.

bout – A short amount of time in which an activity takes place.

calorie – A measure of the energy value provided by foods.

circumnavigation – Sailing all the way around the world.

commemorate – To remember and honor a person, event or achievement.

dribble – When a ball is taken past opponents with slight touches of the feet (soccer) or with continuous bouncing (basketball).

false start – When the start of a race is not allowed to continue because a competitor has started too soon.

Grand Slam – The winning of a group of major championships or matches.

Guinness World Record – The best performance in the world in a specific skill or sport ever recorded by the book *Guinness World Records*.

landmark – A place that is easily seen or recognized from a distance, helping someone to find out their location.

martial art – A sport or skill which began as a means of self-defense or attack, such as judo and karate.

mast – A tall upright post on a ship, often carrying a sail.

navigate – Plan a direct route using instruments and maps.

Paralympics – An event held once every four years where athletes with a range of physical disabilities compete for their country.

point-to-point – A horse race set over a cross-country course.

spectator – A person who watches at a race, game or other event.

sponsor – A person or organization who provides money to an activity or project being carried out by somebody else.

stamina – The ability to keep doing a physical activity over a long time.

steeplechase – A horse race with ditches and hedges as jumps.

WEBSITES

See bossaball in action: **http://www.topendsports.com/videos/tag/bossaball/**

Get caught up in the excitement of an Olympic curling game: **https://www.youtube.com/watch?v=oqE2qfQTHk8**

Here's some competitive rope climbing in the Czech Republic: **https://www.youtube.com/watch?v=dwkaEMiwxCo**

Find out how to skip like a boxer: **https://www.youtube.com/watch?v=GRStBO6uhgE**

Find out more about frog jumping here: **https://www.youtube.com/watch?v=uTJAsZP2iLk**